Tales From a Dead-End Paradise

A collection of ten new
and revised short stories from
The Wigan Pier series
by Ted Dakin

This book is dedicated to my late wife, Barbara and to all those who suffer from dementia.

Ted Dakin

Contents

THE LATE ESCAPE 5

THE TEN STONE CLUB 13

LIZZIE COLLINS, BIRDWOMAN 22

THE SINGING MINER 29

THE SUIT 34

"THE BONES OF THE DEAD" 40

ADOLF'S SPY 48

FAG-ASH LIL 56

A STITCH IN TIME 64

MY DAD WAS A COWBOY 76

Tales From a Dead-End Paradise

THE LATE ESCAPE

I was last in the queue. Everyone before me had gone off with painful expressions, blowing on stinging, painful fingers or rubbing smarting bums. No one escaped punishment. The headmaster, known to us as 'Owd Jack', took a glance at the sheet of paper on his desk and then looked up.

"Name?"

"Dakin, sir."

"Where've you been, Dakin?"

"Broke my wrist, sir, my right one."

" You decided to stay off school?"

"I couldn't do any writing or sums, sir, so Mam sent you a note with Andrew Jones, sir."

"Andrew Jones?"

"Yes, sir. He's in Mr. Lavin's class, he lives just round the corner from us, sir."

He took another glance at the paper.

"You've been off quite a while, Dakin."

"It was broken badly, sir, I fell off an air-raid shelter, they had to put plaster of Paris on, I couldn't write or anything, sir."

Owd Jack stood up. He picked up his cane and came to the front of his desk. He rested the cane against his right shoulder like a rifle. I took a step back.

"Hold out your hand, boy!"

I did so. As he raised his cane to strike, I lowered my arm to soften the blow.

"Higher, boy!"

Tales From a Dead-End Paradise

The pain was acute, agonizing.

"Do you want the other one, boy?"

"No, sir."

Regular offenders swear that it is always best never to change hands; that perseverance and a gritting of teeth was best, that the numbness that followed would eventually deaden the pain. After four more swishes the punishment stopped; but the pain went on. Those regular offending clever dicks must have been telling bloody lies, or wearing gloves.

"Right, laddie, go and report to Mr. Lavin."

With my aching, painful right hand tucked in my left armpit, I made my way to Mr. Lavin's classroom and met another casualty. Tommy Slater, using his desk lid as a cover had been caught by Lavin playing with his didger. Everyone called him 'Tommy Slater, masturbator'. He was always at it.

I had missed morning prayers and thankfully, Mr. Lavin's lesson that morning was poetry readings, which gave my damaged digits a chance to return to normal. The midday exodus for dinner and playtime was a welcome relief. Our school didn't have a flagged playground like normal schools, instead it was was a stretch of dirt, potholed and littered with bricks and broken bottles. We called it the 'Broo' and the teachers, especially Owd Jack, prowled amongst us like prison guards, on the lookout for anyone misbehaving. If Owd Jack collared anyone at fisticuffs they usually finished up doing battle in his classroom, Standard Six. He supplied the blood stained boxing gloves and they supplied the blood; which was always good entertainment for him and his bloodthirsty class, who urged the battlers on to the bitter end.

Saint Joseph's Catholic school, ironically named 'The College'

Tales From a Dead-End Paradise

by us, the disillusioned, desperate collegians, was a formidable run-down place, where even the most backward of pupils were shunted through each classroom, right up to school leaving age. One of these was Ralph Bart. Ralph was in my class and was a seriously, mentally deficient lad, who was never taught to read, write or do his sums. But Ralph was good for a laugh. On many occasions, Owd Jack brought Ralph to the front of the class and was made to perform a childish, Irish jig, by gripping his lanky forelock and doing twirlarounds while singing this made-up, simple ditty:

> I CAN DO A TWIRL-AROUND
> I CAN DO A JIG
> I CAN DO A TWIRL-AROUND
> JIG, JIG.

All done to amuse our headmaster and his class. Another extremely slow-witted lad, Teddy Crowther, suffered far more ridicule than even Ralph. Teddy had actually left school and had found work as a delivery boy for a local firm that supplied stationery goods; pens, pencils, erasers and exercise books, to schools of all denominations. Teddy rode shot-gun in their delivery van, but did all the lifting and carrying, and was in his element doing so. Unfortunately, a delivery to his old school proved disastrous. On this particular day, proud Teddy dumped his parcel of exercise books on Owd Jack's desk and turned to leave, but our headmaster, pretending to show interest in his quarry's welfare, stopped him in his tracks, and moving in close to his victim could smell tobacco on his clothing, Teddy was ordered to turn out his grubby pockets and brought forth packets of wartime foreign fags – Pasha, Passing Cloud and Camel. Teddy, now a wage-earning, ex-pupil, was given a taste of Owd Jack's cane for bringing the school into disrepute.

Not one pupil could escape the evil eye of our headmaster. Not even at weekends. Sunday was church day and everyone had to attend. Owd Jack always attended 10 o'clock mass and between prayers and hymns his eyes missed nothing nor no one. Other mass times were attended by his staff, and every Monday after morning prayers, a roll-call targeted every pupil who had dodged his religious obligations. And there was one thing for sure, if you went to church and were also a member of his rugby team, you could do no wrong. Gerald 'Gerry' Kellerman, didn't play rugby, but he was still a favourite pupil. You see, Gerry was an altar boy and everyone knew that Gerry's greatest ambition in life was to become a priest.

We left school together, did Gerry and I, he to enter a college or seminary (I don't know which) to pursue his priestly ambitions, but Gerry failed. Mentally, he wasn't strong enough to cope with the gruelling demands required and he suffered a nervous breakdown, and his aspirations were shattered. Meanwhile, my ambitions were a little more down to earth. I always had this urge to work with wood (I still do) carpentry, joinery, call it what you like, as long as I was making joints, nailing nails, screwing screws. I don't know where this desire had come from. It certainly wasn't in my genes. Mam had once been a milkmaid and a clerk. Dad had worked with animals, killing them and cutting them up. Anyway, I walked the streets, knocking on doors and joining the dole queues, but it was hopeless. I was getting desperate. Mam wasn't too happy either. She wanted me from under her feet. Any job would do. Brain surgeon, standing on a street corner in short pants, with a tin cup. Anything, as long as I was out of the house.

Then one Sunday afternoon, it came to me, just like the pro-

Tales From a Dead-End Paradise

verbial 'bolt from the blue' I was going to be a writer! At that time Dad used to read a popular weekend magazine and I was casually leafing through the pages, when, Wham! Bam! I saw this advertisement. The magazine was asking for unpublished writers to submit a short story of not more than 500 words, and with a Christmas theme, and with just one winner collecting £50 prize money. I thought, God! This is it. Even with my limited knowledge and education, surely I could write a story of 500 words. And if I did, God! There would be no limits to my literary ambitions. Novels, fame, a mention on the wireless, book signings, people stopping me in the street, and best of all, I would be rich! I couldn't wait. All I wanted was an idea. Something exceptional that had never been done before. But what? Unbelievably, it was Ashton's tobacconist shop situated in our town centre that sparked my creative brain cells.

For a lad, I was a great windowshopper, and one of my favourite windows belonged to Ashton's, Wigan's most popular tobacconist. I could not pass the place. One Saturday afternoon, oblivious to the throng of passers-by, there I was again, gazing in wonder at their fantastic display. Exotic gold-tipped cigarettes, black cheroots, cigars, pipes, tobacco pouches and ashtrays, gleaming silver cigarette boxes, music boxes and, an assortment of chrome and silver lighters. And there it was! Nestling right there on a bed of blue silk was my inspiration, my answer to literary fame, a silver cigarette lighter that had been fashioned into the shape of a small pistol. My heart leapt. There was my plot. There was my story. Dream-like I nipped into Woolworth's, bought 2 ball tipped pens and a thick exercise book and went home. That night I could hardly sleep, and rising early went to early mass. That afternoon, after our usual Sunday dinner of Lancashire hot pot, veg, and red cabbage, I sat on the arm of Dad's easy chair and using Mam's Singer sewing machine as a desk, began to write. The plot sprang to life. This is a synopsis of my story:

It's the week before Christmas and this newly married, childless couple are each secretly fretting about what present they should buy. One evening, after work, the husband, an office worker, visits this popular tobacconist shop intent on buying his wife (a moderate smoker) a cigarette case. Whilst waiting his turn to be served, he spends time gazing into their glass display counter and sees this unique lighter that is in the shape of a small gun. The shop empties, the man, asks to see the lighter, which, when the trigger is squeezed, activates a flame from the barrel by which a cigarette is lit. The man is delighted. Not only will his wife be pleased by this extraordinary gift, but it will also be something to be admired by their friends and a topic of conversation. He makes his purchase, puts the gift in his overcoat pocket and prepares to leave. Suddenly, a rough looking character comes barging in brandishing a cosh and orders the trembling shop assistant to hand over his takings. At this point our hero of the story takes action. Removing the gun-like lighter from the box, he aims it at the would-be robber, who panics and flees for his life. A story of the incident appears in the local paper, with photographs of him and his wife.

And that was it! I rewrote it in my best handwriting and made sure there were no spelling mistakes and sent it off. And then waited ... and waited ... and waited. I didn't get a reply, not even any form of acknowledgement. Today, after all these years, I still can't believe it wasn't accepted. The only conclusion I have come to, is that my masterpiece got lost in the post. We all know what our postal service can be. And besides, it was Christmas time. Ah well!

With all my literary ambitions now dashed, I just gave up, but I

Tales From a Dead-End Paradise

didn't want to join the never ending dole queue and forever tripping over Mam's feet. Alas, it was Dad who found me work. It was one Friday night after tea. He was reading the now extinct Wigan Examiner, when he gave this little exultant eureka shout. Apparently, a local family run saddlery and leather goods business were in search of an apprentice, and Dad (the swine) with Mam's approval (obviously) suggested I was just the lad they were looking for, and like an idiot I agreed to give it a go. But first, I had to get through the interview. I should have smelled a rat. On Monday morning, dressed in my best togs, and a quiff in my brilliantined hair, I was spot on time. But there was no competition. There I was, The Lone Ranger, even Tonto was missing. Sadly, I got the job and suffered for two long years. The owner, a religious fanatic, made outstanding, beautiful harnesses, handbags, belts, and brief cases, but trusted no one, especially me. Just like his Dad, his only son could work wonders with leather. But he was different. He was a black marketeer, who dealt in nylons to foodstuff, and liked his snuff and always gave me a tip for running errands. I liked him. But after two long years, even his pally ways couldn't keep me tied down. I wanted to spread my wings, and soon got them clipped. I found work at a local dairy, had an argument with the foreman and left.

It was about this time that I joined the Wigan Boys' Club. One Thursday night I got the shock of my life. There he was, my old schoolmate, Gerry, standing toe to toe in the club's boxing ring, throwing punches at a lad big enough to be his Dad. Gerry lived t'other side of town so our paths had never crossed, so it was good to see him again. Later, over glasses of sarsaparilla we had a good natter. He never mentioned his failed attempt at his 'Holy Joe' aspirations, and we parted company promising to meet up again. Which we never did.

Tales From a Dead-End Paradise

A few months later, in 1949, the Kings army beckoned, and I was collared to do my two year stint of compulsory army service. I was trained to kill, but never left the country. But I did hear on the grapevine that Gerry, another war office victim, had been posted to Korea to fight in the war between North and South. Out of 90,000 British soldiers who served, there were over 1,000 casualties. Although I never saw Gerry again, I do believe that he survived the conflict along with fusilier Maurice Micklewhite (better known as Sir Michael Caine).

And I survived. Sort of. Fortunately, after my spell in khaki, I got a labouring job with the then Wigan Corporation Water Department, digging holes and helping to repair a variety of burst water pipes, and incredible though it sounds, this was how I came face to face with 'Owd Jack' again. The gang I worked with had been rushed off to a suspect burst main that was causing some road damage, a couple of streets away from my old school. The problem was soon sorted, and about 4.30 in the afternoon we were backfilling the excavation. I was just taking a breather (leaning on my spade, actually) when 'Owd Jack' himself came into view; as he approached, I remembered with clarity, his obsessive rants to all school leavers:

"If you see or pass me on the street, I will expect a smart salute and a 'Hello, Sir', is that understood? A smart, crisp salute, no slouching, is that clear?"

He drew level. Our eyes met. I never flinched. I stared him out. Oh, he knew me all right, even in my mud caked overalls and mucky hands and face, he knew me, but he didn't get that bloody salute or any verbal acknowledgement. No way!

And that was the day I stood defiant. I had finally conquered my fear of a man who for years had dominated, and ruled, by fear and ignorance. It was a late escape. But it felt good.

Tales From a Dead-End Paradise

THE TEN STONE CLUB

Even as a lad, James 'Jammy' Tomkins was a cocky, vain, streetwise opportunist who never missed a trick. In other words, he could always make something out of nothing, especially money. If opportunity knocked, Jammy was in like a ferret. You see, Jammy was a child of difficult and penurious times, and being born to parents who had nowt gave him the incentive to rise above his humble station in life.

It all began with jam jars. Can you imagine anyone making money from discarded jam jars? Jammy did and that's how he inherited his title, Jammy as in jam jars and Jammy because he was always lucky enough to make money from his various enterprises.

Although his mother tried her best, food of real sustenance was in short supply, so, like everyone else in this penniless paradise, jam and home-made bread were constant companions on the dinner table. Jam was cheap, jam was good, and spread nice and thick on doorstep-thick slices, it became a fine staple belly-filler. Strawberry, blackberry, raspberry, plum and apricot; you name it and it was greedily devoured.

It was Jammy's Dad who first gave him the idea. It was one Friday teatime and Jammy's mother had just replaced yet another empty jam jar with a full one.

"It makes you wonder about glass, doesn't it?" Mr. Tomkins said. Jammy's mother plunged a knife into the shiny, succulent contents.

"In what way?" she asked.

"Well, just think about all these jam jars and pickle jars and the like, being thrown int' dustbin."

"What about it?"

"Well, surely somebody should put them to good use."

"I suppose somebody does, but I don't know what for."

"Surely glass factories manufacture more jars and bottles from discarded ones ... they must do. Then there's glass eyes and glass whatnots to be made, the world will always need glass, surely."

"What's glass whatnots?"

"You know what I mean."

Jammy, who had been listening intently to all this banter, butted in.

"Doesn't the rag-and-bone man collect them, Mam?"

"No way, they all get chucked int' bin, he collects other stuff that nobody wants, but he doesn't get much round here." She laughed. "Not likely."

Once the meal was over, Jammy raided their dustbin and retrieved several empty jars, washed them thoroughly and stacked them in their outside lavvy for safety. The following day, instead of his usual visit to the cinema, Jammy borrowed a couple of his mother's shopping bags and walked the streets, knocking on doors, begging for unwanted jars from inquisitive tenants. Soon, with his bags filled to overflowing, he returned home and after a lengthy spell at the sink scouring his sticky collection with hot soapy water, put them with the rest.

It was later that day when Jammy, after trudging two miles with a bulging sack of sparkling clean jam jars slung across the crossbar of his battered bike, finally made it to the yard of a scrap merchant who, after a few tentative questions and an agreement for a further transaction, handed over a substantial

Tales From a Dead-End Paradise

payment to a very delighted Jammy. And that was just the start of Jammy's business ventures. There was no stopping the lad. Door to door work was his forte, and his next project was just as lucrative.

Back then, when coal was an essential commodity, timber too played a vital part in firing-up those ubiquitous coal fires, and Jammy, seeing an opening in the market for kindling wood, moved in fast.

If there was timber to be gathered, by honest means, or otherwise, Jammy helped himself. Once split into kindling, and neatly bagged, Jammy, using his granddad's wheelbarrow for transportation went from door to door and street to street selling his wood to anyone who was interested, and that meant almost everyone. Once again, Jammy, the schoolboy tycoon, was buying Post Office saving stamps for a future that looked promising. But as we all know, the future is never far away and a promising one is usually paved with potholes. "Time flies" his Dad was always saying, and fly it did. At forty-two, Jammy was an unhappily married man with one son who, fed-up with his relentlessly bickering parents, had flown the coop leaving them both wishing they could turn back the clock. But there's only one way to turn back the clock and that is by remembering, and Jammy, forever the optimist, was forever remembering and the more he read the newspapers and watched television, the more he thought about what used to be and how to bring the past forward.

One night, he and Doris, his nemesis, the woman who had been put on this earth for the sole purpose of causing him aggravation and stress, were watching one of those endless TV adverts that guaranteed every overweight woman (and man) a successful formula that would shed those unwanted pounds for good.

"Utter rubbish!" Jammy said.

Doris, who was just enjoying her fourth chocolate biscuit, took another sip of coffee.

"It may seem like rubbish to you," she said. "A man who's never been a pound over 10 stone since leaving school, but some poor sods out there are desperate."

"When I went to school no one bothered about weight or weight loss, they just got on with living best road they could."

"Anyway, why is it rubbish to want to lose a bit of weight, eh?" Doris said.

"Do you honestly think that starvation diets and aerobics will pave the way to perpetual slimness? I don't think so."

"Like I said," she continued, giving him a withering look. "For someone who has to wear shoes in the shower in case he slips down the plug-hole ..."

"Now, now Doris, no need to dramatize ... anyway, I have my own theories about losing weight."

Doris drained the last of her coffee, switched off the television, and said. "Right, doctor clever clogs, how do I go about it?"

"First, you have to be honest with yourself. Have you put on weight?

"Yes, doctor, I have put on a few pounds."

"Good, now you've got to think positive."

"What, no aerobics? No jogging? No dieting?"

"Diet, yes, but first you must diet the mind."

"Diet the mind?"

"Diet the mind and the body will follow."

Tales From a Dead-End Paradise

"Easier said than done, doctor."

Jammy tapped his head. "Everything comes from here."

"Oh, no it doesn't, a cold, a cough, a pain in the backside doesn't come from there, so that quashes that theory."

"I'm talking about positive things, things that come from the power of positive thinking."

"You've been reading too many books."

"You can never read too many books, Doris ... now listen to me will you?"

"Yes, doctor."

"Lesson number one, never, ever plan your meals, don't plan what to eat or how much."

"But ... "

"Listen, a healthy mind and positive thinking means a healthy body, a diet-trained mind removes temptation. For example, remove that biscuit tin and temptation is removed."

"I'll put it in the cupboard."

"Put it in the dustbin."

"That's a bit severe, isn't it?"

"That's only the beginning; cleanse the mind and clean out the kitchen cupboards and fridge of all the food you enjoy that in your own mind you know you shouldn't be enjoying."

"Then what?"

"You replace the food you like with food you're not very fond of."

"That's stupid."

"Don't you see, because you don't enjoy this food you won't

eat as much and hey presto! Your weight will plummet."

"And what about you?"

"What do you mean? I don't need to diet."

"But how can we live like that, me starving myself to death, and you ... well, what will you live on if I've dumped the food we like to eat?"

"We? I didn't mention we, we're talking about you."

"And what will you be doing, doctor?"

"Well, the money we save on food you won't be buying I'll spend it on myself, on something that's a little more up-market."

"Such as?"

"Oh, fresh salmon, partridge, wine, you know ... I might even dine out occasionally."

"While I suffer in silence, eh?"

"You've never suffered in silence, Doris, the day you go silent, I'll know you're dead, anyway that's what you want, isn't it, to shed a few pounds?"

"You're not helping much, are you?"

"Oh, but I am, I've just given you a plan of action that I guarantee will work and if you want to join the 10 stone club, you'll do it."

"You hate me, don't you?"

"How can I hate you when I'm trying to help you slim and recapture the bloom of youth?"

"But it's the way you want me to do it, you want me to suffer."

"We all have to suffer to make gain."

"But I'm not gaining, I'm losing."

"Yes, that's the whole idea, as I've just said, you're losing to regain your youthfulness and the body of a woman much younger than you actually are, and if it works with you I'm planning to go into business."

"What kind of business?"

"I would think that's obvious, you'll be my star pupil for a weightloss plan that can't fail; just think, Doris, you'll become a celebrity, you could even end-up on the television."

"Do you think so?"

"Everyone will be clamouring to become a member of a unique club; the one and only, 10 Stone Club."

"So, that's it."

"That's what?"

"You're still living in the past; money on the brain."

"What do you mean?"

"You're back to when you were a snotty-nose kid, making money from glass jars and firewood."

"How did you know about that?"

"Your mother told me and she also told me what a cocky, arrogant little sod you really were."

"Never! My Mam would never say that about me."

"And now you want to use me the same way, for your own ends."

"Now then, Doris."

"Cocky! Cocky! Cocky!"

"All right, all right, forget it, now are you with me or not? If so, and if we make a success of it, I'll make you a partner."

"That's good of you."

"We'll start off slow, with posters on library walls, in newsagents and chip shops, just think, love, fame at last, women will envy you, and men will lust after you ... Well, is it a deal or not?"

"No!"

"No? But why? We can't go wrong."

"It wouldn't be a very wise thing to do."

"But why?"

"There's only one club for me and I've already become a member."

"What club's that then?"

"The pudding club ... I'm pregnant."

"Pregnant! But you can't be, you're too old."

Doris patted her stomach.

"Not according to this little person, I'm not."

"You're a cruel woman, Doris."

"Who, me?"

"You've let me go on and on and now you tell me there's another little Jammy on the way, that's proper cruel, that is."

"There's no more Jammy's coming into this house, in fact, your Jammy days are about to end."

"And it's put the kibosh on my dreams of a 10 Stone Club, too," Jammy said.

"Exactly, your dream-times will be a thing of the past."

Tales From a Dead-End Paradise

"I don't get that."

"Believe me, dear husband, you will, you will."

"C'mon, then, out with it."

"Well, I've just ordered a cot and two single beds, and when the baby arrives, the cot, and the baby will be in your room, right-up close, to your single bed, so close, you'll hear every whimper, and burp and cry and puke, you'll wonder how someone so small and helpless, can be so bossy and noisy and be the cause of so many sleepless nights."

"And where will you be while all this is going on?"

"Me? Why, I'll be sleeping in the other bedroom having sweet dreams about what might have been."

"Such as?"

"Oh, you know, dreaming of fame and fortune, of envious females and lustful men, and my name up in lights advertising this wonderful club."

"What club?"

"It'll be a night club; The Ten-Till-Two Club actually, but don't worry, I'll not be doing anything naughty, at least, I don't think so, but later when I've regained my figure and my ... er, youthfulness, who knows what will happen, but for now pass me that biscuit tin and while you're at it, I'll have another cup of milky coffee."

Tales From a Dead-End Paradise
LIZZIE COLLINS, BIRDWOMAN

They we're happy enough were the Collins family. Just the three of them, Lizzie, Sid and Bobby, all nice and snug in their smart bungalow on the edge of town. Actually, Bobby was a canary, but he was still an essential part of the family. He was a grand looking bird. Perched there in his brand-new cage, preening his yellow plumage, he could melt the hardest of human hearts; except one.

Sid Collins had come to hate him. You see, Bobby was mute. Bobby had never given Sid, nor Lizzie (who loved him dearly) the pleasure of listening to one tiny, melodious note. Not one twitter or trill even, and, although Sid was philosophical and confident, Lizzie was worried. She loved that bird to bits and to her, a silent canary, was an unhappy canary and, in some strange way, the bird and his wife's supposition, challenged Sid's authority as master of the house. Lizzie wanted to take Bobby to a vet, but Sid resisted.

"I'll get him to sing," he said confidently.

"There may be something wrong with Bobby's vocal cords," Lizzie paused. "If that's what you call them."

"Don't be daft, woman, a bird's a bird, all birds sing, or squawk, trill, twitter or warble, that's what they're made for."

"But ..."

"Leave it to me, woman, we always kept songbirds and budgerigars when I was a lad."

And that is when the rot set in. That once happy, loving home became (for Lizzie, anyway) purgatory. For a woman of her disposition, gentle, kind and thoughtful, the very thought of Bobby suffering like a confined, feathered prisoner was enough to send her insane. And it didn't help matters when Sid began to hover around the cage like a cardigan-clad bald eagle, with permanently pursed lips, whistling tuneless tunes through the bars, singing, chanting and talking incessantly and making all sorts of funny noises. However, Bobby, in silent response, just cocked his little head to one side and seemed to treat Sid's lamentable efforts with dignified distaste. To Sid's credit, though, he never gave up. He even changed Bobby's brand of seed and bought him a celluloid friend in the futile hope that these additions would make the bird happier and more robust. But it wasn't going to happen. Silence reigned and birdbrain Bobby remained aggravatingly tuneless.

So, a now desperate Sid reverted to more desperate measures. In other words, that bloody bird would have to earn its feed.

"Sing for its supper, call it what you like, Lizzie, but I'll make that bloody bird sing even if it bloody well kills me."

And poor Bobby was starved. Sid put him on a diet of tap water. No feed, no seed, no rewards of cuttlefish bone and tasty titbits. Nothing! But all this cruelty began to take its toll on Lizzie's health. She couldn't sleep, she lost her appetite and she began to lose her hair, and while she and Bobby got weaker, Sid seemed to grow stronger and more determined.

It was the actor, Burt Lancaster, who gave Lizzie the idea. It was the run-up to Christmas and, as usual, the TV channels were chock-a-block with film repeats, and this year was the turn of that fine prison film, *The Birdman of Alcatraz*, with Burt's character playing mother to a bunch of sick and ailing sparrows. To see that big, wonderful man hold those tiny, poorly sick birds in his huge hands, to feed and gently nurture them back to chirpy good health, was a wonder to behold.

Tales From a Dead-End Paradise

So Lizzie, in the darkness of her bedroom, while Sid snored his way through the night, plotted and planned and marvelled at her own ingenuity. The following day while Sid went off to collect his pension, Lizzie, her mind now razor-sharp with intent, did a little rummaging and found the object of her search, Sid's brand-new dropper and the appropriate ear drops, she had purchased for Sid's bunged-up ears, and which the deaf sod had never used.

"I'll go and have them syringed at the doctors," he had said.

But that was weeks ago and he still hadn't been, and was still missing half of what she was talking about. But now she was glad. Sid's pigheaded attitude would give Bobby the life he deserved. Bobby was her responsibility now. She knew without doubt that Bobby's survival depended entirely on her healing hands. She knew if she didn't take immediate action Bobby would surely die by the cruel hand of her ruthless husband, and she knew that, ironically, Sid's neglected dropper would save Bobby from certain death. But she couldn't surreptitiously feed Bobby any seed, the evidence of this would be all too obvious. No, there was only one way.

December 15th was a cold, freezing morning. Lizzie, reluctant, but determined, slipped out of bed, leaving Sid snoring audibly – he wouldn't have woken to a brass band playing that American marching song, *Dixie*. She went downstairs, removed the cover from Bobby's cage, warmed a little milk, flavoured it with a smidgen of Sid's best brandy, and filled the dropper. Bobby, unprepared for any kind of force-feeding and intrusion, fluttered and dodged, until a persistent Lizzie, with a quick, but gentle grab and grasp, managed to capture him and force her elixir of life down his neck. Bobby, now subdued and with obvious enjoyment, opened his beak wider and wider, until,

Tales From a Dead-End Paradise

much to Lizzie's delight, the dropper was drained empty. And so it went. Every morning before Sid surfaced and every night after he had gone to bed, Lizzie dutifully fed a now very happy (but still mute) canary her lethal concoction, and Bobby, the only alcoholic bird on the planet, would be waiting with beak wide open for his next session. Sid, however, blissfully unaware of Lizzie's deceit and Bobby's pickled innards, continued with his harsh treatment, but Bobby, who could now barely grip his perch, just ignored him and waited expectantly for his daily cocktail of milk and brandy.

Then disaster struck. On a late return from some Christmas shopping, Lizzie found Sid lying dead at the foot of Bobby's cage, his now dead lips still pursed together, whistle-like, making it all too apparent that he had died as he had predicted, except for one thing; whistling, singing, chanting Sid was indeed dead, but Bobby was still mute and very much alive. With Sid now gone, Lizzie brought out the birdseed, the cuttlefish bone, his little silver bell and his celluloid playmate, but Bobby wasn't interested. Now a fully-blown alcoholic canary, Bobby, denied of his daily cocktail, became silently aggressive, strutting along his perch and on the bottom of his cage, his little gimlet eyes glinting madly.

Then, late one afternoon, in a fit of uncontrolled anger and passion, Lizzie finally realized that her dear little Bobby had become a totally unruly, violent pipsqueak who, to get his daily tipple, began to throw seed through the bars, viciously attack his celluloid friend and rip up his sandpaper. Lizzie watched in horror. Whatever had become of her beautiful canary? Surely he wasn't missing her cruel husband? With Sid gone she had envisaged a long and happy relationship. She wasn't concerned about his silence. It would, of course, be nice to hear a few

Tales From a Dead-End Paradise

melodious notes, but it wasn't to be, Bobby was mute (and frustrated too, apparently) and neither she nor anyone else would ever make him sing, tweet or trill and, although somewhat disappointed, Lizzie had come to accept the situation. But what about these tantrums from her darling pet?

What did it all mean? What would Burt Lancaster have done? Sid would have probably have wrung Bobby's neck, but not Burt, Burt would have brought out his special potions and drip-fed Bobby back to health and sanity. And that's what she would do. Without further ado, Lizzie cleaned-up the mess and put Bobby back on his special diet of milk laced with brandy. She smiled, being partial to a tot or two herself, Sid's best cognac was a bit on the low side. Anyhow, once again peace and tranquility reigned. Twice a day, Bobby, with beak wide open in greedy expectation, took his medicine like the pie-eyed, alcoholic canary he had now become.

On Christmas morning, Lizzie had a lie-in. There was no need to rush. There was only Bobby and herself to care for. At 10 o'clock she went downstairs, made a pot of tea and toast, prepared Bobby's morning medicinal and padded into the living-room, she opened the curtains and removed the cage's cover. Bobby, with beak wide open, waited expectantly.

"I've made you a little extra while it's Christmas, Bobby."

And Bobby, still under the influence from the night before, downed the lot. Then, just as Lizzie was closing the door, Bobby, now completely bladdered and legless, did an acrobatic swing, left his perch and plunged head first to the bottom of the cage as dead as a dodo. Lizzie cried out in dismay.

"Bobby! Bobby! What's the matter, Bobby?"

But Bobby was gone. Now definitely mute – and lifeless – his

Tales From a Dead-End Paradise

boozepickled body had finally succumbed by too much of the hard stuff administered by a naive Lizzie, whose faith in Burt Lancaster (who knew what he was doing) had proved disastrous. Lizzie, now weeping buckets, picked up a fast stiffening Bobby and placed him in her still warm tea cosy with the futile hope that, with a little warmth, Bobby would rise like the Phoenix from the ashes. But, of course, nothing happened and Lizzie was left wondering what to do with a little feathered corpse. She wanted with all of her heart to remember Bobby as a beautiful, active and sometimes naughty canary, who, apart from her husband's wicked intervention, had given her many hours of happiness. But who would have thought, to lose a husband and a pet in a matter of days. Poor Sid. After all, he had only been doing what he had thought best.

I suppose he was right really, a bird, especially a canary, was made to sing. There was no chance of that now, was there? With Sid in the cemetery and Bobby in the tea cosy. Oh, dear! She wiped away her tears, made a fresh cup of tea and sat at the kitchen table deep in thought. There was only one thing to do. She would bury Bobby with Sid. Theirs hadn't been a good relationship, antagonistic, really; Sid with his set, stubborn ways, and Bobby unable to do Sid's bidding and suffering because of it. At least, back in the cemetery, they would lie in peace together and forever. It will be a reunion really, and that will be a fitting end, won't it? She decided to make her next visit to Sid's grave in the New Year. How very nice that will be, to be reunited on New Years Day. Lovely.

So Lizzie put Bobby in a freezer bag and placed him gently amongst her frozen sausages, bacon, the odd pieces of steak and pork chops, but well away from the chicken drumsticks.

Early on New Year's morning she took him out and popped him

Tales From a Dead-End Paradise

into the tea cosy. Indeed, a thawed Bobby would be a nicer looking corpse, of that there was no doubt at all. And Sid too, would appreciate that as well. A determined Lizzie, armed with her garden trowel, a pot of artificial flowers for Sid, and a now fluffed-up Bobby, encased with his silver bell and a brand-new celluloid playmate, inside her best, elaborately carved trinket box, went to the cemetery. At the foot of Sid's grave she made a neat, but deep hole for Bobby's remains.

"He's come to join you, Sid," she whispered. "Our little feathered pet has come to stay with you."

And softly singing 'All Creatures Great And Small' she replaced the soil. Then she paused and listened intently. A strange and wonderful thing happened; a kind of eerie silence had fallen, she was almost sure that all the birdsong and the twitters and the trills had, just for one brief moment, come to a respectful stop. Lizzie looked around.

"You'll love it here, Bobby, among your own kind, and just think, they'll all be singing the songs you could never sing. Now won't that be nice?"

"Yes, what a lovely place this is, Bobby," she said as she turned to leave. "You'll really love it here."

"Well, goodbye, Sid, goodbye, Bobby," she added with a little giggle. "I'm off home now to polish off the rest of that brandy."

And she left the cemetery with a noticeable spring in her step.

Tales From a Dead-End Paradise

THE SINGING MINER

Albert Crabtree was a miner. Daily he laboured, ripping coal from the bowels of the earth; but on Saturday nights he put on his best suit and became a star.

Lancashire bred, Albert's ambition was to move on; to escape from his rented terraced house, to one of quality; to one with a bathroom, indoor toilet and a garden in which to cultivate and to relax on fine summer days.

"And I'll sing us theer," he often said to Brenda.

Because every Saturday and Sunday, Albert Crabtree put on his best suit and sang. Pubs on Saturdays, clubs on Sundays.

Advertised as the 'Singing Miner,' Albert was a natural. With not a singing lesson to his name his tenor voice was out of this world: and when questioned about this gift, his clichéd remark was legendary.

"I do me trainin' in't lavvy."

And every Saturday evening he did just that. With braces dangling and shirt open to the waist, he would amble down the yard to their outside toilet. Once inside, his renditions were awesome. His voice, rich, clear and melodious, echoed with hair-raising clarity into the surrounding streets. An hour later he would be on his way to honour a booking.

His popularity was such that people would travel miles to be thrilled by his magnificent vocalism. Charabancs would be turned away as clamouring fans packed the building. And Albert thrived on it. He attracted females like a matinee idol. And no wonder. His vibrant voice, good-looks and muscular physique held them spellbound, and he in turn became a willing victim of female adoration.

Tales From a Dead-End Paradise

Brenda Crabtree loved her husband so much, there was no love left for anyone or anything. Childless and an only child of parents now dead, she saw to her husband's every need. She didn't work because Albert's demands wouldn't allow it. On Saturday nights while Albert was doing a concert she would slip next door and have a chat with old Mrs. Brown, but never failed to be back home for Albert's return. With his slippers and supper all set out, they made a happy contented couple.

On some mornings when she found lipstick on his shirt collar, her heart bled; but she never complained. She was afraid of the outcome. Besides, where would she go? What could she do? She'd made her vows for life and that was it. However, each night while Albert slept, she would slip out of bed, kneel in prayer, and ask The Good Lord for guidance.

* * *

The envelope. was blue, and it arrived one Monday morning. It was addressed to her.

"That's strange," she thought. "Who would write to me?" The letter was brief and to the point:

MRS CRABTREE, PLEASE HEED THIS WARNING. YOUR HUSBAND IS A WOMANISER. I GO TO MOST OF HIS CONCERTS AND LIKE MANY MORE ADORE HIS SINGING, BUT SOME WOMEN HAVE NO SHAME. ONE ESPECIALLY, A HUSSY IF EVER THERE WAS ONE, SITS AT HIS RESERVED TABLE WITH HIM, AND LEAVES WITH HIM. BEWARE, MRS. CRABTREE AND TAKE IMMEDIATE ACTION.

The letter had no heading and was unsigned.

Confronted now by stark reality, Brenda went into shock.

Housework forgotten, she sat down and wept, dried her tears, thought long and hard and cried again. Somehow, this timid, devoted woman found the inner strength to come to a decision.

That night while serving Albert his tea she propped the letter against his cup.

"What's that, luv?"

"It's mine," Brenda said.

"I can see that," he retorted.

"Read it, Albert!" she exclaimed.

The tone of her voice startled him. He took out the letter and read it. Rubbed his chin and read it again.

"You don't believe this ... this rubbish, do you, luv?"

"And why shouldn't I?"

"Because it's somebody with a grudge ... Jealous of me success, her husband's run off with another woman ... Who knows?"

"It's not true then?"

"Course not, luv."

"What about this woman sitting at your table, and leaving with you?"

"That'll be Connie, Connie Consort, we're a double act sometimes."

"And what about the lipstick I find on your collar?"

Albert laughed.

"Oh, that, some of the audience get carried away. You know what women are like."

"I don't like it, Albert."

Tales From a Dead-End Paradise

"Look, Brenda," Albert waved the letter about. "All this is bunkum. It's all made-up lies."

"There's only one way to find out," Brenda said.

"Er, what way's that, luv?"

"I'll come with you, Albert, every booking you have I'll be with you."

"But you don't drink, luv ... and besides, what will you do when I'm on stage?"

"I'll be singing, Albert."

"Eh? What do you mean singing?"

"Singing, with you, Albert. Singing duet."

"Flamin' 'eck! You can't sing, Brenda, you'll ruin me."

"Mrs. Brown, next door thinks I've got a lovely voice."

"Uh! Mrs. Brown's old and decrepit, and as deaf as a post, how would she know?"

"My mind's made up. I'll leave you to do the organizing. By 'eck I'm getting quite used to the idea. I can see the billing now."

She raised one hand and spread her fingers.

"The Warbling Crabtrees. What do you think, Albert?"

Never thinking for one minute that Brenda would carry out her threat, Albert did nothing. She didn't have it in her, not Brenda.

* * *

And so, in a tense and uncomfortable atmosphere, time passed by. One Saturday evening, early in March, Albert downed his usual light tea and headed for the back door. Even in stressful times, Albert never broke his ritual.

"How do I look, Albert?" asked Brenda.

Tales From a Dead-End Paradise

She was standing at the bottom of the stairs. Her dress, which Albert had never seen before, glittered and sparkled like a Christmas tree.

Albert cleared his throat.

"Going out, luv?"

"Tonight's the night, Albert. Just think, The Warbling Crabtrees, we'll send them wild."

Like a man in a trance, Albert went down the yard, entered the lavatory and closed the door. A minute later that rich and sonorous voice echoed with a haunting beauty, from yard to yard, from house to house. Never in all his singing days had Albert's voice reached such a crescendo. Neighbours stood spellbound, waiting in awe for that final top note. But it never came. Those haunting words ended in a strangled gurgle. Albert's mighty voice was no more.

* * *

On medical advice, Albert gave up his weekend singing, and with it went his lust for living. His ambitions for a better quality of life were drowned in the sorrows of his failure.

Brenda, knowing that she had been the cause of her husband's breakdown, never forgave herself, and her guilt drove her to the spiritual comforts of the chapel. Albert, too, realizing the need for guidance, became a Christian, and with his wife became an ardent supporter of many religious activities.

And with this transformation came a miracle. Albert began to sing again. Every Sunday morning his powerful voice can be heard in hymnal chorus, leading the church choir.

THE SUIT

Where I lived in the 1930s, everyone was poor; and it showed. Rented houses with one cold water tap, outside blocks of dilapidated closets, and a dull, unvarying diet. But the biggest give-away of this dire existence was blatantly obvious. Armies of clones trudged our cobbled streets, men in dark creased jackets, baggy trousers and cloth-caps. Women wearing clogs and shawls, and kids dressed in long-sleeved jerseys and short pants. Everyone looked drab and colourless.

To ease domestic pressures nothing was thrown away. Children's clothing was passed down through the family brood. So that's how it was with poor folk. Make do and mend, pass it on, hand it down. There was no end to it.

Our John was far too young for hand-me-downs, and me being the one and only big brother had never had any. Not until Mam received that brown paper parcel from Canada.

Mam was an avid writer of letters, and her frequent correspondence to her sister in Nova Scotia were usually replied to with some small gift. Woollen mittens, socks, and the odd scarf, I must admit, were all very welcome to a family who had nowt.

Then one Friday in October 1937, that brown paper parcel arrived.

"Here, Edward," Mam said, "try this on."

"What is it?"

"A suit. It's come all the way from Canada. It's a good 'un too."

"Do I have to, Mam? I was goin' out with me mates."

"Not before you've tried this on you're not."

Tales From a Dead-End Paradise

It was no use arguing, but at this particular time of the year, collecting bonfire wood was about the most important thing in the world. The suit wouldn't fit. I struggled and grunted like mad as I tried to squeeze into it. The trousers were so tight, I feared castration. The jacket too, rendered me incapable of any free movement. Mam's gaze was one of unconcealed admiration.

"Ooh, it's lovely ... I bet it cost a lot of money."

There was no doubt about it, the material looked and felt expensive. The jacket had patch pockets, broad lapels and five buttons. The trousers, complete with leather belt, had no turn-ups, and sported, not one but two hip-pockets. The brown, small check pattern, caught in the glow of our evening fire, had a sheen that comes, not from wear, but from quality.

"I'm not wearin' it," I said defiantly.

"What! ... What do you mean you're not wearin' it?"

I began to sweat pounds and moved away from the fire. I tugged at the jacket.

"It's too tight, Mam, it's killin' me."

"Don't be daft, it fits like a glove."

I fumbled with the belt and blew hard.

"Soddin' hell, Mam it's two sizes too little."

"There's nowt wrong with it. Leave the jacket unbuttoned. And if you swear again I'll clout you one!"

"And what about these, eh?" I tried my best to lean forward.

"Look, these pants are too short, I look gormless."

"I might be able to lengthen those a bit."

"And what about here?"

I forced my legs apart and indicated the region of my genitalia.

"I won't be able to pee."

"Cheeky monkey ... Many a lad would go crazy for a suit like this."

"I'll go crazy if I don't get it off, and quick!"

"I want you to keep it on till your Dad gets back. Sit down, he won't be long."

"If I do, I won't be able to get up."

"Sit down and stop exaggerating."

Just then in walked Dad carrying our John. On seeing me standing to attention, red-faced and sweating buckets, he nearly dropped my brother on his head.

"Flamin' 'eck, what's up wi' 'im?"

"What do you think, luv?"

"I think he needs a doctor."

"What do you think about the suit ... the suit?"

"Tell her, Dad ... tell her it's too little."

Dad laughed.

"It's either that, lad, or tha too big."

"Stop jokin', Dad, and tell her."

Dad took a closer look and turned to Mam.

"Put it this way, if the lad breaks wind he'll take off like a flamin' sky-rocket."

"Right, that's it. Off it comes, I'm wearin' it no more."

"It'll be all right with a few alterations, you'll see," Mam insisted, unperturbed

And I did see. Even after Mam's expert needlework, the second try-on was just as bad. But Mam remained adamant.

"It'll be a crying shame if it's not worn," she said firmly.

I decided to play on Dad's obvious sentiments. With Saturday's weather still consistently fine, Dad, a fresh air fanatic, set off for a countryside walk. I kept him company. We had just crossed Elston Bridge when I made my move.

"I hate that suit, Dad."

"I don't blame you, lad."

"You don't?"

"I must admit, I think your Mam's gone a bit too far this time."

"Then why don't you tell her?"

"Because we've got to bide our time, lad. That suit's come all the way from her sister in Canada, she'll feel guilty if you don't wear it."

"And what about me, eh? I'll be the laughing stock of Mayflower Road."

"I know ... I know, leave it to me, I'll think o' summat."

Then Mam dropped another of her bombshells

"Your Dad's taking you and our John to visit Auntie Beatrice on Sunday, and I want you to wear your new suit. And no excuses!"

The threat of that simple statement once again sent me into a well of deep depression. In desperation I looked across at Dad reading his newspaper. What had happened to his promise?

"Leave it to me," he had said. Uh!

My only consolation was, Auntie Beatrice lived only three miles away, and the shortest route was along the canal, over the river Douglas, and through some fields.

As we crossed the canal a boatee on a horse-drawn barge gave us a friendly wave. A few minutes later we left the towpath and tramped through tall grass to a second bridge that spanned the stinking, foul waters of the River Douglas. The closer we got the stronger the stench.

Halfway across the aged wooden bridge, our John, overcome with a sudden fit of adventurism, broke away from Dad's grip, made an unsteady dash for the other side, tripped, fell and rolled like a human ball under the bottom rail and into the shallow, weedy water below. Dad, without hesitation, climbed between the rails, hung momentarily from the structure, and dropped close to his struggling infant. Panic stricken, I ran from the bridge down to the water's edge. Dad, holding our John above the foul smelling river, was making slow headway through the water and slime towards me.

"Throw mi summat, lad, quick!"

I grabbed the branch of a nearby bush and tugged for all I was worth; but it was hopeless. There was nothing else for it. Off came the jacket. Keeping a firm grip of one sleeve, I waded out as far as I dare and flung the coat towards them. Dad, stretching out his free hand, managed to grab the other one.

"Well done, lad, now pull like hell! Go on, pull!"

Slowly, but surely, they both made it to the bank.

On arriving home, Dad led us down the entry and into the backyard. A lift of the latch and a shout for help soon had Mam

Tales From a Dead-End Paradise

hurrying to the backdoor. After the initial shock of seeing her whole family slime-covered and smelling foul, she went into action. Within twenty minutes she had our John washed and changed and shining like alabaster.

One hour later, with the three of us spick and span and smelling strongly of carbolic soap, Dad gave her the full story.

"Oh, I'm going to have quite a job getting our Edward's suit clean, I must say."

"And what about my clothes, and John's," said Dad, seizing the moment. "What are you goin' to do with them?"

"Oh, they'll have to be thrown away."

"And why is Edward's any different? Besides, that suit'll fall apart before you get rid of that pong."

"I suppose you're right, but it's a crying shame ... a good suit like that."

Dad gave me a crafty wink.

"I know, luv, but these things happen."

Every year, we, the Mayflower Road gang, took pride in building the biggest and best bonfire in the whole area, an honour we once again achieved. And to celebrate this annual, boisterous occasion, Mam produced an enormous tray of treacle toffee, and I was given the job of making sure everyone received a fair share.

What a night it was. Whizzers, bangers and rockets flashed and zoomed, and hot roast potatoes were consumed, while high above us, in my suit, sat the best Guy Fawkes that Dad had ever made.

Tales From a Dead-End Paradise

"THE BONES OF THE DEAD"

I looked back and saw Grandad, hand on tiller, framed against a dying sun, looking for all the world like a figure of doom. Ahead, in the oncoming twilight, I could see the familiar dark and looming mills of Wigan. I sighed and gave Jenny's bridle a gentle tug.

"We won't be long now, girl, we'll soon be home."

The mare, sensing my mood, shook her head and snorted, sending clouds of vapour into the cold, clear air.

Grandad was a boatman, who for some forty-odd years had made a living hiring out his boat; to carry anything from coal to cotton, from anyplace to anywhere. Now, the hiring was over, we had made our last delivery. The Zulu and Jenny where up for sale, which left Grandad's future prospects somewhat bleak, and me, his new apprentice, jobless.

Years earlier, the trading of cotton, coal and other goods, had relied heavily on many local waterways, which prompted Grandad to take a gamble. Within weeks he had become the proud owner of a horsedrawn narrow boat. Cotton from the mills and coal from the surrounding pits, and Grandad was in the big time. For years all went well. Then disaster struck. The steam train took over. The age of speed had arrived. Slowly, relentlessly, the canal trade went into slow decline, and Grandad made his all-consuming decision, and headed for Wigan.

Once through Paxton Locks, the smoking stacks of our neighbourhood came into view. A few minutes later, with the Zulu safely secured and Jenny unhitched, we led her from the canal bank towards home. The path took us past Jack Calman's factory, known locally has the 'boneyard' whose wordy sign announced to one and all:

Tales From a Dead-End Paradise

J. J. CALMAN AND SON. SUPPLIERS OF SELECTED COWHIDES.

THE FINEST GLUE AND GENUINE BONEMEAL FERTILIZER.

We hurried on, trying in vain not to inhale the unholy stench which was a permanent reminder of their produce. As we went along, a rickety wagon piled high with the bones of many slaughtered cattle, rumbled past.

"The bones of the dead," said Grandad, solemnly.

We crossed Gambler's Field which linked Calman's factory to the very cobbles of Mayflower Road. At the corner, where snot-nosed kids played under a gas lamp, we parted company.

The following Sunday, just after tea, with Mam knitting and Dad round at Grandad's, we had a visitor. Father Dillon, our parish priest, was doing his rounds. As usual, he was on the lookout for lapsed Catholics and collecting money for the town's waifs and strays. With another tanner in his collection bag, he settled down in Dad's armchair and nibbled on a biscuit.

"Well, young man, how's life down on the canal?" He smiled broadly. "What a life, eh? Plenty of fresh air and honest to goodness toil, what more can a man ask for?"

"It's over," Mam said. "Over and done with, Father, Grandad's selling up."

"Selling up? Goodness me, you must be devastated."

"Which brings us to the question of money, Father."

"Money? I don't understand."

"We'll need every penny now, there'll be none for the church, I'm afraid."

The cleric gazed into his teacup for a while, then looking up said.

"Do you know a Mr. Kyle, young man?"

"You mean, Amos Kyle, the rat catcher?"

"That's the chap ... well, I do believe he's on the lookout for an apprentice, but seems to be having problems."

"No bloody wonder," I thought.

"Could you put in a word for the lad, Father? He'll be ever so grateful, won't you, love?" Mam said.

"No, I won't," I said.

Ignoring my lack of enthusiasm, the priest eased himself out of Dad's chair.

"I'll give him a visit, anyway and get him to call on you, is that all right?"

And before I could agree or disagree, he lifted the latch and was off like a ferret.

True to his word, on the following morning, Amos Kyle was at our house, scoffing Mam's home-made cake and discussing my future. Amos, the only rat-catcher for miles around, was employed by Jack Calman on a regular basis. Apparently, Jack always demanded immediate action, which wasn't surprising. Bonemeal, which Jack sold as crop fertilizer was made from powdered animal bone; it was the firm's main produce. Rats loved the stuff and thrived on it. So it was left to Amos and his dog Dinky, to kill as many of the vermin as possible. Between more bites of cake and noisy slurps of tea, Amos gave me a brief outline of what was going to be my first ratting expedition.

"We'll start tonight at midnight," Amos said.

"Tonight?" I replied, "but it's Friday."

Tales From a Dead-End Paradise

"Rats can't tell the time, lad, and we'll have all weekend to collect our tails"

"Tails?"

"Aye, tails, that's how Jack Calman pays me, a bob a tail."

"A shilling? That's not much."

"It is if you catch enough."

"That means a lot o' rats," I said.

"There's a lot o' rats to be caught, lad, and Calman's no fool, he wants prove o' puddin', so to speak."

At midnight prompt, armed to the teeth with clubs, traps and Amos's patent rat poison, we made our way to Calman's factory. As we crossed the muddy yard, Amos briefed me once again as to his proven methods. It was Dinky's job to flush out and kill as many rats as possible; the ones lucky enough to escape his savage fangs, would fall victim to our clubs. Once the physical onslaught was over, traps would be set and poison pushed down the many infested tunnels that ran under the premises, the poison, inducing tremendous thirst would force the rats to surface, and where they would die an agonising death. The next day tails would be lopped and added to the ones we had caught the night before.

At the door of a half-timbered warehouse, Amos whispered his final instructions.

"The dog goes in first, then you, I'll switch the lights on ... you go left, I'll go right, right?"

"I think so," I quavered, "but ... what do I do next?"

"Bloody hell! I've told you once. You see a rat, you clobber the bugger, right?"

"Right."

Slowly, without a sound, he opened the door. Dinky, needing no command, bounded off into the darkness. With my heart racing out of control, I followed. In the sudden glare of light, I froze. Dinky was nowhere to be seen, while Amos, already on the run and club at the ready, flung out an arm.

"Down there!" he shouted. "Left! Left!"

The fertilizer, ready and bagged, was stacked into neat regimented rows. I ran down a narrow alleyway and skidded to a stop. In front of me, dozens of the devils were feeding on meal that had spilled from the sacks. Rooted to the spot, I waved my club timidly. Suddenly, Dinky, muzzle smeared with blood, bounced into view. The rats trapped between us and sensing death, took the better option and scurried towards me. Humpbacked and squealing like mad, they closed in. I was petrified. One ran over my foot, Dinky bit into it, shook it and pounced on another. Galvanised into action, I struck out, strongly, accurately. A kind of madness overcame me. Skulls cracked and bodies were pulped under my lethal club. And on it went.

I was acting way out of character, but the power of death over this scurrying vermin was stimulating and euphoric. Eventually the slaughter stopped. Exhausted, but triumphant, we collected the dead. Outside, by torchlight, we set traps and laid poison. My first night's work was over. It was time to go home.

Grandad was still having problems. He couldn't sell Jenny nor the boat. As time went on, Grandad began to weaken. He began to drink. To buy alcohol, he would sell anything. A couple of weeks after my ratting experience, Grandad came calling. His knocking was loud and continuous, and on my opening the door it was quite obvious the old man was upset and agitated. He was holding on grimly to Jenny's bridle.

"I'm glad you're in, lad, I've made a sale, I've sold Jenny."

"That's brilliant, Grandad, who is she goin' to?"

"Will you come wi' me, lad, just for company, like?"

"Course I will, I'll get my jacket."

Mam was still at the table sipping tea.

"I wouldn't go if I was you, lad."

"I think I'd better, Mam, Grandad looks a little upset."

"So he should be, he's sold her to Timpson's t'other side of town, she's being sold off as horse meat, he's having her put down."

"God Almighty!" I cried. "He wouldn't do that, not Grandad."

"It's the only sale he could make, leave it him. Let him do his own dirty work."

"You lied to me, Grandad," I groaned as I returned to the door. "You're taking her to Timpson's to be slaughtered."

"It's the only way, lad, nobody wants her or the boat ... but I never lied to you." He patted the mare fondly and his eyes began to fill.

"It's the only way," he said again.

"All right, I'll go with you some of the way and then come back home."

Twenty minutes later I returned home to find that my Mother had company. Once again, Amos Kyle was doing justice to Mam's home-made baking.

"'ere's me owd mate. Where've you been, lad?"

Mam caught my eye, put a finger to her pursed lips and shook her head.

"Oh, just out and about," I replied.

"Anyway keep thi coat on, lad, we're off to see Calman, it's pay day."

On our way to the boneworks, Amos gave me a friendly pat on the shoulder.

"Listen, lad, I were havin' a word with Jack the other day and between us we've come up wi' a plan."

"What sort o' plan?" I queried.

"Well, Jack's stocked up to bursting point wi' bonemeal an' he's thinkin' about using your Grandad and his boat to do some deliveries, how about that for a bit o' luck?"

"It's a bit late for that, Amos," I mused.

Clearly Amos wasn't listening and continued with the so-called plan.

"The idea is, the owd man will deliver direct, there's many a regular buyer wi' farms close to the canal, so the goods will be taken to the doorstep, so to speak."

"It's too late, Amos," I insisted.

"Too late? Too late for what? What are you goin' on about?"

"Grandad's taken Jenny to the knacker's yard, he's had her put down."

"Put down? You mean ... ?"

"Slaughtered!"

"Bloody hell!"

After collecting our money, I left Amos and Jack deep in conversation. I wanted to get home. I knew without a doubt what the topic would be.

On reaching home, I was surprised to find Grandad sitting on our doorstep.

"What're you doin' here, Grandad, why don't you go in?"

"Waitin' for you, lad. Where've you been?"

"Collecting me wages from Calman."

"It's good to have a jingle in thi pocket, lad."

"So we're both rich, Grandad; how much did you get for Jenny?"

"I couldn't go through with it, lad,"

"What do you mean?"

"Anyroad," Grandad smiled, "she's back in her stable waitin' for a miracle."

"Do you believe in miracles, Grandad?"

"I've never seen one yet."

"Then hang on to your braces, Grandad, and get Jenny saddled up."

With that, I began to run, back to Calman's as fast as I could!

Tales From a Dead-End Paradise

ADOLF'S SPY

Before the birth of television and high-rise flats, living in as we did, close to a canal, was an integral part of a unique upbringing that nurtured a variety of experiences, never to be forgotten. The excitement of play, the trauma of death, the joy of freedom, and on this odd occasion, the drama of war.

In the year of 1940, while the war raged around us, we, the kids of Mayflower Road, schooled, played and changed our ways not one iota. On winter days, if it was cold enough, our canal became our icerink. On summer days, in the heat of the sun, the canal became our swimming pool. And this was one of those days.

The sun was high and strong and the irresistible deep, dark coolness of our canal drew us like a magnet to its murky depths. When me and my big brother, Tom, reached Elston Bridge the place was alive with white, goose-pimpled, naked bodies. Close by the bridge, opposite Walton's foundry, a line of moored canal boats had already become roosting places for a horde of shivering, dripping swimmers. The sound of laughter, splashing, shouting and bragging, was all around us.

"I dare thee dive of yon bridge," said a familiar voice.

It was Sandy Robson. He was as old as me, but bigger and stronger, and a better swimmer. And he knew it.

Elston Bridge wasn't high, but to dive from it was extremely dangerous. Below the bridge was a watery scrapyard. Rusting bikes and prams and bedsteads, and any unwanted sinkable thing was down there, waiting to bruise, impale, or trap any reckless diver.

"I will if thy does," my brother said boldly.

"Don't be daft, Tom," I said, "tha'll break thi flamin' neck."
Undaunted, our Tom ignored me.

"C'mon, Robson, thee go first and I'll follow."

Everyone had jumped off the bridge, but to dive from it was almost suicidal. Sandy climbed through the wooden rails and stood poised on the edge. He looked around, grinned, and dived without hesitation into the murky depths below; surfacing almost immediately, he began to tread water, and in a taunting voice, shouted.

"C'mon, Tom, are tha scared, o' what?"

My brother, not to be outdone, did his dive and surfaced beside him, gasping, grinning and spewing foul water. I ran down the bank to help them out.

"How about from the top rail?" Sandy said.

"Suits me," Our Tom said. "I'm game if thy is."

Once more, our Tom and Sandy were the focus of attention. I shaded my eyes against the glare of the sun as Sandy, once again, brimming with confidence, dived with Tarzan-like grace from the top rail, and entered the water like a spear.

I held my breath, as Tom, with obvious nervousness, climbed onto the top rail. Just at this moment, two lads on a makeshift raft made from oil drums, floated slowly under the bridge. Our Tom, seeing them, teetered like a drunken man, found his balance, and launched himself. His style was loose. His dive was wrong. He hit the canal with a loud, ominous splash, just missing the two would-be sailors.

"That weren't much flamin' good, was it?" shouted Sandy, still treading water and obviously pleased with himself.

We waited for Tom to surface. Nothing happened. I looked up

and down, searching for his face among the many swimmers. No Tom!

"He's havin' us on." Sandy said. But his smile was false as if frozen on his face. After what seemed forever, I began to panic.

"He's in trouble, Sandy, something's up. Go down for him. Please, Sandy, 'urry up!"

Just then, up popped our Tom, just like a cork, spluttering, coughing and blinking, his hair plastered to his head like a black skullcap.

"I thought you'd had it, kid." I shouted.

He swam towards me and held out his hand.

"Give us a hand-up, Ted," he pleaded.

As I pulled him out, Sandy gave us a wave and swam off to one of the canal boats.

"I thought you'd had it, kid," I repeated.

"There's summat funny down there, Ted."

"What is it, a body?"

"Don't be stupid!"

"What is it, then?"

"It looks like a parcel, it's in a pram."

"A parcel? What's wrong wi' that? There's all sorts in't cut."

"When I went down I caught me shins on this pram, then I saw it ... this oilskin parcel lying in the pram ... I think there's summat in it."

"Why didn't you bring it up?"

"What, and let Sandy Robson and the flamin' lot o' them see what it is? Not flamin' likely."

"But it might be nowt at all."

"We'll soon find out," he exclaimed, and with a swift look around, cocked up his backside, and vanished from sight.

After what seemed ages, he surfaced clutching the mysterious package in his right hand.

Minutes later we crossed Elston Bridge and hurried past the narrow footpath which led to the rear of Walton's foundry. As a precautionary wartime measure against any attack from the canal, the Ministry had erected two massive concrete blocks and a sentry-box which was manned by the Home Guard.

When we reached home, Mam was out. Dad, though reluctant to put aside his cowboy book, listened to our story. After some hesitation, he untied the oilskin bag, and slowly, carefully, removed a pistol. He examined the gun with great care and rubbed his chin.

"By 'eck," he enthused, "it's a German Luger."

"How did it come to be in the pram?" I asked.

"By chance probably. Somebody must have thrown it from Elston Bridge," he suggested.

"Is there any bullets in it?"

"Luckily for you, no."

"Why chuck away an empty gun?"

"'cos a gun's no use wi' no bullets, that's why." Tom said.

"Could there be a German livin' near us, Dad?"

"A German, round here? I doubt it, lad. Here, take it to the police station, hand it in, and tell them everything you've told me."

Out on the street, Tom grabbed me by the arm.

Tales From a Dead-End Paradise

"Listen, Ted, you might be right."

"What about?"

"About a German bein' round here. After all, who would want to get shut of a German gun, eh?"

"I think you're right, anybody else would hand it in, just like we're doin'."

"But we're not handin' it in, Ted."

"We're not?"

"Supposin' this, Ted, supposin' there is a German, a German spy, and he's on one of them canal boats."

"What would he be doin' on one o' them, Tom?"

"Spyin' on Walton's foundry, it's a place where stuff's made to help beat Germans."

"But why should he have an empty gun?"

"How the hell should I know, I don't know everything, nobody does."

"I was only askin'."

"Anyroad, he doesn't need one if he's only sendin' messages ... he could send some sort o' signal, disappear, and the place could be bombed."

"But what can we do about it?"

"Reet ... we keep the Luger, then toneet we'll do a bit o' spyin' of our own. Are you with me, kid?"

"If you say so, Tom," I replied warily.

Later that night, while Mam and Dad slept, we crept downstairs, and guided by a full moon ran across Gambler's Field, and onto the canal towpath, as we approached Walton's Foundry,

Tales From a Dead-End Paradise

I gave my brother a nudge.

"What about the guard?" I ventured.

"Let's hope he's havin' a cuppa," replied Tom.

But it wasn't to be. The glow of a cigarette-end from the shadow of the sentry box, told us different.

"What're are we goin' to do now?" I asked anxiously.

"I don't know," replied Tom curtly.

"Let's go home," I suggested and made to turn away.

"Shh ... just a minute ... what's that?"

A few yards along we could see a makeshift raft rocking gently and tapping against the canal side. We climbed aboard the drums, lay belly-down, and using our hands as paddles, propelled our way across the water. On reaching the opposite side we hugged the canal bank, floated past the sentinel, and came to a stop a few yards short of the first craft. We tiptoed across the towpath and went down into Three Corners Meadow.

"What do we do now?" I said.

"Look for somebody signallin', you idiot."

I knelt on the grass and gazed intently at the shadowy outline of boats. Not a glimmer. I began to get restless.

"But, who will he be signallin' to?" I asked.

"Flamin' Germans, who do you think, stupid?" Tom retorted. "C'mon, we'll have to get closer."

As we reached the towpath, Tom came to a stop and held up his hand. He pointed to indicate the nearest barge. I held my breath and listened. There was no sound, but a chink in a curtain showed us a glimmer of light from within. Once again we went into our tiptoe routine. With heads close together, we looked inside. Seated at a table was a British soldier playing some kind of card game, We watched for a while, then Tom gave my sleeve a tug.

"Let's get the name of the boat and make tracks."

But unfortunately our transport had drifted off. There was only one thing to do. We crossed the bridge and made our silent way towards the sentry box.

"Halt! who goes there?" a loud, officious voice boomed.

I nearly wet myself. I wanted to shout, "friend!" but the word wouldn't come. We turned round, hands above our heads, and walked back towards a tall, uniformed guardsman who was wielding a rifle and fixing us with an accusatory stare..

"Stop! Declare yourselves!" he bellowed.

"We're Tom and Ted," Our Tom announced.

"What're you doing here, this time of night, eh?"

"We've been lookin' for somebody."

"Oh, aye, and who would that be, then?"

"A German spy," Tom said.

There was a long pause Then a chuckle.

"A German spy? Round here? Have you gone barmy?"

"And I think we've found him," Our Tom said, removing the Luger from his waistband and holding it in front of him.

"We think this is his gun."

The guard hesitated, lowered his rifle and took the pistol.

"You'd better come with me to the gatehouse."

At the gatehouse he placed two chairs together and ordered us to sit. He picked up the telephone and dialed a number.

Tales From a Dead-End Paradise

"Can I speak to Detective Colby, please? ... oh, it's you ... This is Bert Wilton speaking, I'm doing guard duty down at Walton's, I wonder if you can come down straight away, there's a bit of a problem ..."

Eventually, Detective Colby made an appearance, and after listening intently, promised a full investigation.

The end result of our wartime adventure came to a rapid conclusion, or so we thought. Detective Colby came in person to inform us of his investigations. Our German agent, it seemed, was a British army deserter. He'd gone absent without leave, six months previous, and had been on the run ever since. But the story doesn't end there.

About six weeks after our spy-hunting adventure, just two hundred yards from Elston Bridge, the bloated body of an unknown man rose to the surface. The blue serge suit he wore was scrupulously examined. Pockets were turned out, and linings checked for maker or vendor. Nothing was found, not even a handkerchief. His shoes too, when scrutinized, also revealed nothing. The man's identity was a complete mystery.

However, when the body was taken to the mortuary and stripped, an astonishing discovery was made. Around his neck, tattooed for perpetuity, was an indelible necklace of minute German swastikas.

Tales From a Dead-End Paradise

FAG-ASH LIL

The death of a spouse can result in devastating consequences, and can affect the surviving partner (depending on the circumstances, and the partner) in a variety of ways. This story concerns just one of them.

Lilian and Billy Sefton, and Billy junior, lived near the bottom of Mayflower Road. Now situated between their house and Calman's bone works, was a brickyard, and it was there the local council dumped tons of broken flags and disused cobbles, to be crushed into fine and coarse gravel; and that is where Billy senior worked, on a large and noisy stone crusher.

Back in the Forties when work was hard to come by, Billy's job was a secure one, and at that particular time, fairly well-paid.

As a small family their living standards were quite reasonable, a little restricted perhaps, but they were happy enough. Just about.

The pleasures of Lily and Billy were limited to Billy drinking like a fish (to wash down the gravel dust) or so he said. And Lily, well, Lily liked a fag, in fact, she liked a lot of fags, and smoked like a factory chimney, and because of her addiction, the residents of Mayflower Road gave her the honourable title of 'FAG-ASH LIL'.

For all their indulgences, the couple kept a good table, possessed modest, but sturdy furniture, and made sure that Billy junior was well shod and decently dressed.

You could say it was a marriage made to last. They very rarely Quarrelled and when they did, soon made-up. It wasn't exactly a marriage made in Heaven, but stable enough, all the same.

With his workplace in close proximity, and Lil – who didn't work – but kept the house spick and span and mealtimes on the dot; what else could one wish for?

It was one Wintry Saturday night when it all came to an end.

With Billy junior outdoors playing some street game, Lil stoked up the fire, made a cup of tea, lit up another fag and settled down to listen to *The Man In Black* on the wireless.

A knock on her front door made her curse. The policeman standing there apologised, and after confirming her identity, asked could he step inside.

"Would you like to sit down, Mrs. Sefton?"

Everything about him, his ominous presence, his bulk, and the tone of his voice, spoke of doom.

"Why?" asked Lil, leaning against the table. "What is it? ... what's wrong?'

"I'm afraid it's your husband, Mr. Sefton ... he's had an accident...'

"Accident? Accident? Where is he? What's happened? What kind of accident?"

"I'm afraid, Mrs. Sefton, your husband is dead."

"Dead? But he can't be, he's gone into town for a drink."

"That's where it happened, as he was leaving the Black Raven pub in the town centre. Apparently he tripped stepping off the kerb and fell under the mayor's car. Killed instantly, I'm afraid."

"The mayor's car?" Lil exclaimed incredulously and too shocked to cry. "Was he driving?"

"The mayor doesn't drive his car, Mrs. Sefton, he has a chauffeur to do that for him."

"But where was the mayor's car going so late on a Saturday night?"

"Apparently he'd just left some sort of function at the town hall and was on his way home."

Lil took another drag from her umpteenth cigarette of the evening.

"What am I going to tell our lad, constable? This'll kill him."

"You'll have to tell him the truth, you can't hide anything like this."

"Poor Bill, poor lad ... poor me," Lil lamented as her eyes began to moisten.

"Would you like me to stay while you fetch the boy?"

"No, no, I think it better if we're alone."

"As you wish, Mrs. Sefton."

The constable replaced his helmet and adjusted his cape.

"You'll have to make a formal identification, of course, but someone else will be making contact." With that he touched his helmet and bade her goodnight.

"By the way, constable," said Lil, "how do you know it's my Billy whose been killed?"

"The landlord of the Black Raven knew your husband well, very well, in fact."

"Oh ... I see," replied Lil with a sniffle. "Well, goodnight constable and ... thank-you."

As an only son, young Billy took the death of his father better than expected. The father and son relationship was basically non-existent. As a family they never went on holiday, and when Billy senior had finished a hard days graft at the brickyard, his only thought after tea was sleep, which he did every evening in his comfortable armchair. An hours kip, a wash and brush up, a change of clothes, and off he went on his usual pub crawl till closing time. On returning home his son would already be tucked up in bed, and in his own dream world. His wife, Lil, however took his death very badly. It wasn't just the physical and psychological circumstances of his demise; it was the aftermath. The lack of physical contact, his non-presence, the emptiness ... the empty purse.

Yes, after a period of settling down came the realisation that with Billy's death, her weekly income had also diminished. Regrettably, they had never saved for the proverbial rainy day.

"How are we going to manage?" she found herself uttering on more than one occasion

They did manage, just about. A cut back of this, a cut back of that, a cut back of fags! And that is the one thing, Lil could not bear, a cut back of that very essential consoling weed. She had smoked too heavy and too long; she just could not do it. Without a fag she too would die. The very thought made her tetchy and unreasonable.

Oh, why, why had her drunken husband fallen under the wheels of the mayor's car and not head first into the stone crusher while doing his job of work. That way she would have been entitled to a trouble-free, and reasonable pension for the rest of her days. What rotten luck! What had she done to deserve all this?

With the passing of time, Fag-ash Lil's fears became a reality, and her daily quota of cigarettes became ever scarcer.

In a desperate attempt to keep puffing, she resorted to the humiliating act of going on the cadge. She would walk the streets or stand at her front door begging from neighbours, passing workmen, even strangers. To satisfy her craving, she began to plot and scheme and Billy junior, who loved his mother and sympathised with her sufferings, became her salvation.

Since time began, women knew that the way to a man's heart ... and his mind, was through his stomach, and although Billy junior was just a lad, his mother used that same age-old ploy.

It was one Friday teatime when she set her plan in motion. Armed with the biggest dinner plate she could find, she went round to Gregson's fish and chip shop. First in the queue, she ordered a large cod, a double portion of chips, and not one, but two scoops of peas. Then across the road she went to Mrs. Weatherall's corner shop and bought the biggest cream cake on display.

Young Billy, just like his Dad used to do, rolled up his sleeves and made his attack.

"It's not my birthday, is it, Mam?" Billy enquired eagerly.

"Don't be cheeky, course it's not," Lil replied.

"Well, what's the occasion, then?" he continued.

"I just thought I'd give you something special, that's all."

"Thanks, Mam, this is really good, thanks!"

After tea, and with Billy still feeling replete, Lil took a long, deep drag on her cigarette.

"Do you still love your Mam, Billy?'

"Don't be daft, Mam, course I do," he replied.

"Then would you do something special for your Mam, lad?"

"Anything, Mam, anything at all."

"I don't like to ask, Billy love, but things are getting really serious."

"What is it, Mam? What do you want me to do?"

Tales From a Dead-End Paradise

"You know I like a fag, don't you lad?"

"Everybody knows you like a fag, Mam."

"And you know that since your Dad died we ain't got much money."

"Well?"

"Well, I'd like you to start collecting fag-ends for me."

"Collecting fag-ends?"

"That's right. If you keep your eyes open you'll see plenty on't pavement and in't gutter."

"And you want me to start collecting them?"

"Yes, but don't step in't roadway, I don't want you ending up like your poor Dad."

"And what will you do with them?"

"I'll break them open, collect all the tobacco, and roll my own."

"That's really desperate, Mam."

"These are desperate times, lad ... I can buy cigarette papers for next to nothing; they even sell little machines with rollers."

Billy pondered her proposition for a few moments.

"OK, Mam, I'll do it. Anything for you." he confirmed.

Fag-ash Lil – with a lot of help from Billy – went back to being a happy woman. Friends and neighbours gave a sigh of relief.

In those days, long ago, it was a well-known fact that Whitsuntide Monday was the day that Roman Catholic schools and churches held their annual Walking Day. Dressed specially for the ocassion, the congregation followed massive banners of their faith. Bands played loud, rousing tunes, and grateful spectators lined the streets to watch and applaud in response to a very moving spectacle.

Now Fag-ash Lil and Billy were not of the Catholic faith, but Lil persuaded young Billy to take part and join the walkers.

"Just tag on at the tail-end, lad," she said, adding, "nobody'll know any different, and just imagine the fag-ends you'll find. I mean, from start to finish takes hours, all them streets, you'll have a field-day."

Billy wasn't so sure, but when she turned up with a flower for his buttonhole that she had pinched from Wigan Park, the poor lad hadn't the heart to refuse.

Billy was away for four hours, and when he returned he had not one solitary fag-end to his name.

"But what happened, lad, you did walk, didn't you?" asked Lil.

"Course I did, Mam. And I enjoyed it, but I got caught, didn't I?" he explained

"Caught?"

"Aye, Father Brownlow from St. Josephs caught me at it, told me off, made me empty my pockets, and asked why I was doing it ... I had to tell him, Mam."

"Of course you did, lad, that's all right."

"There's something else, Mam."

"Oh?"

"When I'm older he wants me to become a Catholic, and I think I might, Mam. One of me mate's a Catholic, he's an altar boy, an' he's always going on about it."

"That's all right, Billy, you do as you please."

Tales From a Dead-End Paradise

Nevertheless, Billy still did his duty, still collected fag-ends for his Mam and even saved up to buy Lil a brand new cigarette making machine, so that all of his Mam's fags were well-packed and uniform in size and shape.

About six months on and Lil's luck, once again, took an upward turn.

It happened one Monday at midday. A rattle on her front door knocker interrupted her housework. At the door stood a man in overalls, holding an inscribed, shiny black flowerpot, the type used in cemeteries.

"Mrs. Sefton?" the man enquired.

"Yes," Lil confirmed, staring at the flowerpot.

"I've been asked to call round with this 'ere pot for your late Billy's grave ... it's from all of us, his workmates, and boss ..."

"And who are you?" Lil enquired.

"Fred's me name. I got Billy's job on't crusher."

"Oh, you'll have to take care, it can be very dangerous, you know, " she warned.

"That's all right, I'll not be missed if owt happens, anyroad," Fred replied solemnly.

"Not married, then?"

"No, I reckon I'll always be single, who'd want somebody like me anyroad, a labourer on a mucky stone crusher, eh?"

Lil looked him up and down, took a deep, comforting drag on her cigarette, before exhaling a plume of blue smoke.

"Hmm," she said, with a wry smile, "would you like to come in for a cup of tea? I'm just about to put the kettle on."

Tales From a Dead-End Paradise

A STITCH IN TIME

I left school in the Summer of 1945 aged fourteen, when our wartime hero, Winston Churchill, was rejected as a peacetime leader and his successor, Clement Attlee, announced that a period of austerity lay ahead. And boy, was he right.

For the time being however, my escape from a school that taught me very little, was a euphoric occasion and because of the headmaster's ruling that only short pants should be worn by all pupils, my first pair of long ones was an added bonus.

For the first two weeks, Mam gave me the freedom of the streets, then one particular Monday morning gave me a gentle hint that it was time to start looking for work; and that was the problem.

I had this urge to be a carpenter, but numerous visits to the dole and applications to various firms proved fruitless. My desire to become a full-time 'chippy' came to nothing.

It was Dad who first saw the advert; and I remember it was on a Friday evening after tea.

He shook out the evening paper, crossed his legs and from the comfort of his fireside chair, read aloud the following announcement:

BENJAMIN BRISTOW AND SON, MAKERS OF SADDLERY AND FINE LEATHER GOODS, REQUIRE YOUNG, WILLING APPRENTICE. GOOD PROSPECTS GUARANTEED. NO REFERENCES REQUIRED.

Dad put down the paper and gave me a triumphant look.

"By 'eck, that's just the thing, Ted," he declared. "It won't be much money, but it's a trade ... not far to travel, either."

"Where is it?" Mam said.

"Why, near't town centre, not far from bus station."

Tales From a Dead-End Paradise

"That's only about 15 minutes walk, and no bus fares, either.' Mam said. "And like your Dad said, it is a trade, you'll be set up for life."

"How about it, Ted?" Dad said.

"I suppose so ... but if I don't like it I'm not stoppin'."

"I'll come with you, if you want," Dad said.

"Not flamin' likely. What do you think I am, a flamin' kid?"

"Better make it quick, then lad, I bet they're queueing up for a job like that."

'Aye, I bet they are. Anyroad, I'll go Monday mornin' early."

"They'll be open tomorrow you know. it's that sort o' business."

"I'll go Monday," I said defiantly.

"Please thisel."

On Monday, at 10 o'clock sharp, hair neatly parted and slicked back and shiny shoes gleaming black from Mam's assiduous polishing, I made my way through the sun-warmed streets.

I was dreading this interview and hoped and prayed that the job had been taken. The closer I got to my destination, the slower I walked. Then, inevitably, I arrived. The name and business was displayed outside, reading just like the advertisement, with one addition: ESTABLISHED 1899.

Bristow's was housed in a low, nondescript and whitewashed building situated well away from other shops and businesses. I entered through the only visible door.

I then encountered a long wooden counter with a hinged flap, barring my way. All was eerily quiet.

"Hello!" I called out, "is there anyone? ..."

Tales From a Dead-End Paradise

From a dimly lighted rear, a small stout, bespectacled man, wearing a brown apron across his ample belly, emerged and peered at me quizically.

"I've come about the job," I explained.

"I'm Mr. Bristow," he smiled. "I own the place. Come through, will you," and lifted the counter flap.

The pungent smell of leather was almost overpowering. The workshop was untidy. In the centre was a pot-bellied stove, with a tubular chimney going through the ceiling. On the far wall were three unattended wooden benches, littered with an assortment of unfamiliar tools and unfinished work. An aged saddle, a pair of battered, leather trousers, (the kind worn by speedway riders) and an expensive looking brown handbag.

I followed him into a small office on the left. Once behind his desk, he gave me a searching look and smiled. But he didn't smile with his eyes, which were close together like that of a little piggy.

"Sit down, laddie ... sit down," he said, pointing to a small rickety chair on the opposite side of the desk to him.

"What's your name, by the way?"

"Ted, sir" I replied humbly.

"No need to call me sir, Ted, Mr. Bristow will suffice."

"Thank you, Mr. Bristow."

"Now, Ted, what school did you go to?"

"St Joseph's."

"You mean the Catholic school close to Wigan Pier?"

"Aye, that's the one."

"And do you attend church on a regular basis, Ted?"

"We had to, Mr. Bristow, t'headmaster saw to that."

"And now you've left school will you continue to attend?"

"I don't think so."

"Why not?"

I shrugged and replied with an answer that I had given little, if any, consideration to.

"I've done enough church goin' to last me a lifetime."

"I go to church, Ted, regularly ... no one forces me, I just know it's the right thing to do."

Things were getting serious and I found myself shrugging again.

"I'll probably keep it up, Mam and Dad'll probably make me go anyway."

"Good lad. Now, how's your reading and maths?"

On hearing this question I thought it best to do some more lying.

"Top o' the class, Mr. Bristow," I ventured, hoping to God that he wouldn't test my mathematical skills. As it was, he seemed more than satisfied with my reply and seemed very keen to take me on.

"Good, now then, when can you start?" he enquired.

"Is there no one else in for the job then?" I said.

"No, Ted, you're our first applicant."

"Just my bloody luck," I thought.

He rummaged around in his desk drawer and drew out some official looking forms.

"How about starting next Monday? We open at 8:30, that gives us time to get organised for a 9 o'clock start."

"8:30?"

"Yes. And I do appreciate good timekeeping. Understand? In the meantime ask your father to fill these in, please," he said while handing me me two of the forms with something of a flourish.

The following Monday at 8:15 prompt, I was welcomed by a grumpy Bristow and ordered to make a fire in the pot-bellied stove. I gave him the forms Dad had filled in and signed, and then set to work. Kindling wood, newspaper and coal were kept in a metal box at the stove's base. With great difficulty and considerable cursing under my breath, I managed at last to get the thing going.

My next task was to sweep the floor and tidy the workbenches littered with odd-shaped, razor sharp knives, and tools. Then I was shown how to beeswax lengths of thread used for stitching leather.

Later, over tea and biscuits he gave me a general idea of what my working day would be. Mornings would be spent similiar to this one, cleaning up, and tidying benches. Afternoons, I would spend learning the trade; small stitching jobs on leather off-cuts, rivetting and intricate tooling would also be on the agenda.

He pointed to a bench on the far side of the worshop.

"You'll be using that bench over there, the one next to it is mine, that way I'll be able to keep an eye on your progress ... and the other one is Vernon's."

"Vernon?"

"My son, my only son," he explained. "He's on holiday just now ... but he'll be back tomorrow.' Mr. Bristow sighed and shook his head slightly.

Tales From a Dead-End Paradise

"I hope so anyway," he muttered.

From this I sensed that all was not well between them.

"Do I call him, Vernon, Mr. Bristow?"

"Yes, yes, Vernon won't mind ... he doesn't mind much about anything, does our Vernon, but you will find that he's quite demanding."

Vernon Bristow was in fact the complete opposite to his father. Slight of build, with a good head of brown hair that topped a somewhat thin, crafty looking face. He was a likeable person, all the same.

His first demanding request to me came at midday; consisting of obtaining a tin of snuff from a nearby tobacconists and two cold pork pies from an equally nearby butcher's shop. He devoured the pies along with a huge mug of tea while seated at his bench scanning the day's race meetings.

One thing I did notice, was that while his father's work entailed saddlery and harness and general repair work, Vernon concentrated on the more exclusive of leather goods; elegant handbags, purses and wallets, some of them made to customer's specifications.

And me, well, apart from easing myself slowly into this world of leather, I was also the errand lad.

One Friday afternoon, Vernon handed me a brown paper parcel containing a beautifully made shoulder-bag, with a delivery address in the more grander part of town. So, with enough bus fare safe in my pocket, I set off.

Number 3 Armitage Way was set in its own grounds, well away from the bustle and noise of passing traffic. It was a large and imposing property, located at the end of a long driveway which was bordered on each side by mature trees and shrubs. Feeling somewhat intimidated by these grand surroundings, I tentatively rang the bell.

A few moments later, a tall and very attractive woman, dressed in a plain black frock, answered my ring.

"Mr. Bristow ... Vernon Bristow, asked me to deliver this parcel, Miss ... Mrs ... erm," I mumbled uneasily.

She gave a brief smile and then, taking a few steps back, beckoned me forth.

"Come in, young man," she said warmly, "would you like a glass of lemonade, or something?"

"No, thanks," I replied. "I ... I have to be getting back."

"Are you sure?" she enquired as if a little disappointed. "Anyway, just bear with me, I'll only be a moment."

She left the door ajar and I watched as she went over to a table in the hallway and opened the parcel. Scarcely glancing at the shoulder-bag's exquisite leatherwork, she opened it and took out several cellophane packets. Each packet contained what appeared to be silk stockings which she carefully laid aside. I knew that such luxury items in 1945, could only be obtained on the black market.

My heart missed a beat as she returned to the front door with a jaunty step and a broad smile.

"Tell Vernon I am delighted with the goods," she declared.

"He's done a wonderful job. Tell him that will you?" she continued.

I merely nodded in the affirmative.

"And this is for you." she said, shoving a threepenny bit into the sweaty palm of my right hand.

With that, she bade me farewell and closed the door. I then found myself retreating quickly from Armitage Way, knowing that my venture into what for me was effectively unknown territory was at an end.

* * *

As my time as an apprentice continued, I began to feel that Benjamin Bristow seemed overly concerned with regard to my personal life. On one occasion, when neither he nor I were particularly busy, and Vernon was absent, he began what I regarded as an uneasy interrogation.

"You don't smoke or swear, do you Ted?" he enquired with a tone that implied such activities were highly immoral.

"No, Mr. Bristow, I don't."

"Remember, Ted, even when you're old enough, never take to drink, it's the ruination of man ... in every sense," he declared archly.

"And what about girls ... do you have a girlfriend?" he asked, his top lip curling slightly upwards as he spoke.

"No, Mr Bristow," I replied firmly, my intention being to dissuade him from making any declarations regarding sexual morality. "No girlfriend."

An uneasy pause followed, during which I hoped that he would desist from asking me any further questions that as far as I was concerned had little or nothing to do with my my being in his employ.

"Still going to church, are you?" he ventured breezily.

"Of course, Mr Bristow," I replied, still trying to maintain an uneasy balance between, on the one hand, respect for my elder and employer, while on the other, a feeling of dislike for what I regarded as his impertinence.

"What kind of friends do you have, Ted? ... I mean, are they good and decent lads you knock about with?"

"Aye, of course they are," I replied firmly.

"Have you or any of them ever been in trouble with the police?" he enquired, showing no signs of letting up.

This whole situation was becomingly uncomfortably weird and moreover rather tiresome. I was I admit feeling intimidated by him, but was nevertheless determined not to show it.

"Why do you want to know that, Mr Bristow?" I asked, fixing him with as bold a stare as I could possibly muster under the circumatances.

"Just fatherly-like concern, lad. You see, while you're working for me, I'm responsible for your welfare, and your progress ... you're one of the family now," he affirmed.

I wondered what Dad would have to say about that.

Thankfully, the cross-questioning was now concluded as Mr. Bristow returned to his workbench while instructing me to sweep up the back yard.

* * *

During the course of the next few weeks, little stickers began to appear at certain strategic places in the works, especially in the toilet:

"FLEE FROM THE WRATH TO COME!"

"GOD IS EVERYWHERE."

"TRUST IN THE LORD."

I was hoping for some kind of reaction to these rousing declara-

Tales From a Dead-End Paradise

tions from Vernon, but he had other things on his mind.

For weeks, he had been hard at work making a small attache case, and on occasion, I watched spellbound as leather, locks, hinges, studs and remarkably neat white stitching, eventually became the finished product. Also, just to provide a further touch of quality, a deep green cloth lining was lovingly applied. On the lid, in gold inlay lettering, was the name: JOHN. C. BRANDON. Vernon then gave me the job of giving the case its final polish, which I carried out with as much devotion as he had shown to the case's manufacture.

The finished item then stood on a shelf for about a week until one day I realized it had disappeared and Vernon called me over to his bench.

"I want you to do another errand for me, Ted," he announced, handing over another brown paper parcel.

"I want you to deliver this attache case to the same address as last time. It's for Mrs. Brandon's husband ... John, they're old friends and I do special jobs for them, you see."

I accepted the parcel somewhat gingerly, while taking the utmost care not to drop it.

"I'll need some bus fare, Vernon," I said with a grimace.

"I want you to use the bike," he replied. "Dad's been complaining about the time it takes using buses, and by the way, be careful. If you find the case is a little heavy, it's because I've packed it with thick cardboard. OK?"

"I'll take good care of it, Vernon," I said confidently.

"You can have your dinner before you go," he declared, adding, "that way should get to their house about 1:30. You'll have plenty time to check the bike over, you know, tyres and what have you before you go."

"Does Mr. Bristow know where I'm going?" I enquired.

"Er, no, Dad won't be in today," he replied. "And, when you leave, I'll be closing up. I've an urgent appointment in town, so don't hurry back, OK?"

Dinner consisted as usual of a few meagre sandwiches and a bottle of pop, after which, just as I was putting the parcel in the bicycle carrier, Vernon gave me a curt nod and departed.

And later, after a 10 minute chat to an out-of-work mate, who happened to be passing, I too set off. At that time of day the roads were fairly busy and when I reached the town centre there was a bobby on point duty directing traffic.

He gave me the halt signal for a few minutes, then beckoned me forward to which I complied with a wobble. However, just at that moment, I noticed Vernon on the opposite side of the road, accompanied by a shady looking character. As both men then entered the Black Horse public house, I wobbled even more. A few moments later, a car, that seemed to come from nowhere, crashed into me. Fortunately, I managed to fall without injury, and struggled to my feet, after which I noticed to my horror that Vernon's parcel was in tatters under one of the front wheels of the car. Worse still, the once pristine attache case had burst open to reveal its contents. There was no sign of any of the cardboard protection that Vernon had mentioned, but instead those now familiar cellophane packets of nylons, as well as chocolates, and cigarettes and ...

"Well, well ... what have we got 'ere?" the bobby sneered knowingly, making his next question somewhat redundant.

"What's this lot then?" he enquired, picking up the case before fingering its contents with a kind of mailicious delight.

"I think you'd better accompany me down to the station, laddie," he declared with unwarranted zeal, as if he had foiled a major bullion robbery!

At the police station, consoled with tea and biscuits, I told my story. The attache case was confiscated and I was told to go home, heeding the warning that I might be required as a witness at a later date. Vernon would have an official call the following day.

And that call, by a tenacious, young constable, quashed my suspicions of any wrongdoing on Vernon's part. As it turned out, he was found to be innocent of any unlawful misdemeanours. Apparently it was determined to be entirely legal for him to supply his friends, the Brandons, with gifts that were very scarce in those years of austerity, and with me acting as postman. Well – all's well that ends well!

Not long after that bizarre experience, I decided that I wanted a change, something with more of a challenge. After two years of riveting, tanning, and stitching as well as the more mundane tasks, it was time to move on, time to leave it all behind, and remember it all as just ... *a stitch in time* ... so to speak.

Tales From a Dead-End Paradise

MY DAD WAS A COWBOY

Do you remember how many picture houses there were in Wigan's town centre? They've all gone now, leaving in their wake numerous shops, clubs, car parks, a swimming baths and the offices of Wigan Life. However, let's take a metaphorical stroll down memory lane so to speak...

Do you remember the Ritz in Station Road? The poshest cinema in town. It was at this cinema that I first saw *'The Adventures Of Robin Hood,'* featuring the best swashbuckler of them all, the dashing Erroll Flynn as Robin. It was 1938 the same year the film was released.

Just short walk from the Ritz, tucked away up a narrow passageway just off Market Place, was the Empire. I think this was the smallest picture house in town.

Another hop, skip and a jump away, down by the side of The Clarence Hotel, was the Princess cinema. I recall once, (it must have been about 1941, because the blackout was in force) I and a couple of mates went to see *The Curse Of The Wolfman*, a horror film, starring Lon Chaney junior. On our way home one of me mates ran on ahead and hid in a dark recess of Wallgate bridge, and when we drew level he jumped out, screaming like a demented Dervish, with claw-like hands raised above his head. Mam nearly had some extra washing that night, and I'm not kiddin'!

Walk under this bridge, and just past Caroline Street, on the right-hand side, stood the The Wallgate Cinema, but we used to call it The Scratch, because after every visit to this establishment, you were certain to come away itching like mad.

Back up Wallgate again, turn right into King Street and onwards to The County Playhouse that still displays, high above the entrance,

Tales From a Dead-End Paradise

the date it was built, in 1916. I think this was the first cinema to introduce a back row of double seats; ideal for courting couples.

Just a spit away, across the road, was The Royal Court Theatre. The Court to us Wigan peasants. The one exceptional treat for the patrons of this cinema was the electric organ, played by a one-legged organist, that would rise majestically a few feet as he played some favourite tunes before the lights went down, and again in the interval.

Cross the street again, down past the Hippodrome, was The Palace. Now, the Palace had two entrances. One for the front and back stalls and one for the balcony; which we called the 'gods' and which boasted an entrance of several fine marble steps.

Last, but not least, was the Pavilion Picturedrome at the bottom of Library Street. Who can ever forget that splendid ornamental frontage of the 'Pav' as we called it. A facade that belied the rumbustious goings-on inside; especially on the balcony, known locally, as 'The Monkey Rack' That was definitely the place to avoid if you wanted to enjoy the picture.

But out of all these cinemas, the good, the bad and the indifferent; it is the Palace that stays in my memory. I reckon the Palace cinema showed more Western films than all the rest put together. And boy, did I like Westerns. Dad, too, was an avid fan of cowboy films. Nobody loved Westerns more than Dad. Nobody! But Dad's obsession was understandable. And I'll tell you why.

I remember, it was a Sunday morning and Dad as usual was singing a cowboy song. He was always singing them – about cattle drives, gunfights, bank robberies, bar-room brawls. The lot! And, all of them true ... or so he said.

Dad had a good voice, and the lyrics were always catchy and

entertaining, and it was this combination that finally prompted me to ask him as to how it was that he knew so many of the cowboy songs.

He gave me a steady, earnest look before replying.

"The only answer I can give you lad," he said, with a gleam in his eye, "is that when I lived before, I was a cowboy."

"Lived before? What do you mean, Dad?"

"Well, I died ... shot probably ... then I was reincarnated."

"What's reincarnated?"

"Reincarnation means, born again. Rebirth."

"Is everyone born again, Dad?"

"There's some who think so."

"Even Mam?"

"Erm ..." Dad scratched his chin.

Just then, in walked Mam carrying a basket of dirty washing.

"I was just asking, Dad, did you ever live before, Mam?"

"I were just explaining t'lad about reincarnation," Dad explained.

Mam gave him a black look.

"There's on thing for sure, if I do come back, I'm coming back as a man."

My mind was in turmoil.

"But, if I lived before, then who was I?"

More daggers from Mam.

"I don't know about reincarnation, but one thing's for sure."

"What's that, Mam?"

Tales From a Dead-End Paradise

"Nine months before you were born, your Dad had a twinkle in his eye, then you turned up."

"I don't understand that, Mam."

"Your Dad'll explain, won't you, luv?"

Dad looked at her and me uneasily and cleared his throat.

"I'll ... er ... tell you one day, lad."

I was getting more and more baffled and confused. Anyroad, one day Dad's conviction that he had been a cowboy became a convincing reality. Jed Coop's pony, Jimmy, had done the rag-and-bone rounds for many years, until, one hot summer's day Jimmy collapsed and Jed had to put him out to grass. However, within weeks, Jimmy collapsed again and never recovered. Jed, hating the thought of retirement, bought a robust piebald pony and called it Patch. Now Patch had a warm and comfortable stable behind Jed's house, but did his summer grazing on Gambler's Field, which lay behind Calman's bone works and where Dad was employed.

Every day, after doing his rounds, Jed would lead Patch into his stable-yard, unload his cart, give his horse a bucket of fresh water and remove his saddlery, except for his bridle, by which he led the animal down to Gambler's Field. However, on this particular day, the ritual went drastically wrong.

As horse and master reached Calman's factory gate, the 5 o'clock whistle blew. Patch, startled by the high-pitched blast, snorted and reared, causing Jed to lose his grip on the bridle. Patch, now released, set off at a mad gallop, sending several of Dad's workmates diving for cover. Dad (so the story goes) managed to grab Patch's bridle, then moving with some alacrity, made an acrobatic leap onto his back, and with a strong pull and soothing words, brought the stricken animal skidding to a halt. Then it did

Tales From a Dead-End Paradise

a steady canter back to a grateful Jed. To the tenants of Mayflower Road that brave act made Dad a hero and was never forgotten. And, as for me, well, I was now convinced without a doubt, that Dad had lived in another age, in an age of cowboys and Indians and gunslingers, and I was proud of him.

It's a few years now since Dad went to that prairie in the sky, but every western film I watch – and I watch a lot – I always think of Dad and Patch, and begin to make comparisons; not with John Wayne, not with Audie Murphy, and definitely not with Roy Rogers. No, Dad was a dead ringer (so to speak) of Randolph Scott – tall, thin-lipped, steely-eyed and ramrod straight. But even so, it's not Scott who I see riding off into the sunset at the end of a picture. It's Dad riding Patch, bless him!

And now I'm older and wiser, I know too, what Mam meant when she talked about that twinkle in Dad's eye. You see, when Dad was thinking about having me, he knew that he would be siring another reincarnation. Another once-upon-a-time cowboy, someone he could be proud of. Someone to carry on the family tradition. It were that that put the twinkle in Dad's eye, nowt else!

Anyroad, folks, after all this remembering, I'm feeling mighty nostalgic, and in a few minutes time, Channel 5 is showing yet another western. I've seen it before. About 30 times, I think. But I don't care; because I know Dad will be somewhere up there, twirling his six-shooters and singing another cowboy song:

Way down in Texas, back in my home town,
A gang of rustling cowboys they shot my old man down.

Now the man who did this killing, they called him
Trigger Kid, and I swore that I would get him if it was
the last thing I did.
So I joined the Texas Rangers to see what I could do.

Tales From a Dead-End Paradise

The Captain said: "The life is tough, but we're needin' men like you."

There was me and Pete and Lefty, we tracked those outlaws down ... we found them in a bar-room in a outlaw border town.

They shot up Pete and Lefty as they were on the run, so I pulled out my 45'er and I shot them one by one.

The Publisher

This book is published in collaboration with the author by Green Arrow Publishing. We are an independent publisher, based in the North-West of England, specialising in the publication of all types of Fiction, Non-fiction, Poetry and Drama. We operate a Collaborative Publishing Scheme, providing authors with the opportunity to see their work in print and digital formats.

John Dench
Publishing Editor
Green Arrow Publishing